The Cowboy Chuck Wagon Cookbook

Good Eatin' & Plain Talk from the Wide Open Spaces

by Kelsey Dollar

The American Pantry Collection™

Published by:
Apricot Press
Box 1611
American Fork, Utah
84003

books@apricotpress.com
www.apricotpress.com

ISBN 1-885027-18-4

Cover Design & Layout by David Mecham
Printed in the United States of America

Chuck wagon images are courtesy of the Hansen Wheel
& Wagon Shop. Building and restoring horse-drawn
carriages and wagons for over 20 years, Hansen Wheel
& Wagon Shop is the world's foremost wagon builder.
Visit their web site at www.wagons-wheels.com for
more information.

Cowboy photographs are courtesy of Dayton Molzen
and Landmark Photography. For more information,
visit www.landmarkphotos.com.

Forward

I was raised in a wide-open-spaces kind of a family. So, naturally, I'm a wide-open-spaces kind of a girl. All my life, I have rubbed elbows with old time cowboys and ranchers as well as young cowhands. In the areas I have lived, I have been surrounded by horses and pick up trucks, rodeos and roundups, dust and sagebrush, simple wisdom, and terrific cookin'. As a young "cookie," during a round up with my family, I have seen hired cowboys toast Rocky Mountain Oysters on a stick over the fire, although the cowboy delicacy never appealed much to me. I have sweet memories of this wonderful lifestyle, and in my family tradition, most good memories are combined with food.

It has been painful to witness the fading of this untamed way of life. With this cookbook, I want to do my part to preserve a little of the feeling, flavor, attitudes and especially the food of the cowboy. Personally, I love good chuck wagon cooking and chuck wagon living. I hope my efforts will help you experience and enjoy the cowboy way of life.

Kelsey Dollar

Recipes

Cash it in Golden Rod	9
Wyoming Campfire French Toast	11
Chile Relleno in a dish	12
Apple Oatmeal	14
Shorty's Scramble	15
Herman's German Pancakes	16
Lead Pancakes	18
Rise 'n Shine Ham & Eggs	20
Potato Pancakes	21
Dripper Breakfast	22
Stick to Yer Ribs Oatmeal	23
Whole Wheat Pancakes	25

Scones	26
Honey Butter	27
Tiny's Venison Stew	32
Aunt Phoebe's Goulash	34
Rabbit Stew	36
Poor Man's Sausage Soup	37
Texas Beans	38
Traditional Chicken Fried Steak	39
Fernando's Hot Caldo Con Queso	41
Jim-Bob's Noodle Mixins	42
Brian's Dutch Oven Beans	44
Trail Beans	45
Pear Pork Chops	46
Long-Riders' Stuffed Zucchini	49
Old Time Trail Mincemeat	50

Gus' Baked Beans 52

Hank's Pheasant & Mushrooms 53

Will's Scalloped Mushrooms 55

Ellis' Lake Trout 56

Grampa's Deep Fried Fish Fillet 58

Range-Rider Cowboy Pie 59

Dwayne's Famous Meat Loaf 61

Lyin' Around Soup 62

Doc's Dutch-Oven Corned Beef 64

Campfire Trout 65

Oatmeal Venison Patties 67

Cowboy Coffee Can Cake 71

Raid the Hive Honey Bread 72

Cowboy's Cake 73

Annie's Whole Wheat Muffins 74

Six Weeks on the Trail Muffins 75

Frenchy's Zucchini Bread   76

John's Baking Powder Biscuits   78

Chuck Wagon Noodles   79

Aunt Polly's Dumplings   80

Slim's Corn Bread   81

Best Durn Yellow Cake Ever   83

Sugar Cookies For Your Sweetie   84

Betsy's Buttermilk Cookies   86

Bucked Off Banana Cookies   87

Maria's Flan de Carmelo   89

Arroz Con Leche   90

Mom's Raisin Spice Cake   92

Redheaded Cowgirl Carrot Cake   93

Cowboy Cider   95

7 Day Sweet Pickles   97

Big Bull BBQ Sauce   98

Breakfasts

The first one up in the morning
has his pick of the horses.

Cash it in Golden Rod

2 eggs
3 tbsp butter
2 tbsp flour
salt and pepper
2 cups milk
toast or split biscuits

Hard boil the eggs then peel and chop the white and grate the yolk. Melt butter in a saucepan. Stir in flour and season with salt and pepper. Slowly add milk, stirring constantly until it is thickened. Add chopped egg white. Pour sauce over toast and sprinkle with egg yolk.

The cook is far and away the most important
person in any ranching operation.

———◆◆✖◆●———

It does no good to be the fastest draw if
your aim is no good.

———◆◆✖◆●———

It's only because of the cow pie that the
sunflower can grow.

———◆◆✖◆●———

Wyoming Campfire French Toast

2 eggs
1 tbsp milk
cinnamon
6 slices thick cut bread*

*Thick cut homemade bread or Texas toast works best.

Beat the egg and milk together in a bowl. Dip both sides of bread
in egg mixture and cook over medium heat in frying pan until
golden brown, then flip and brown other side of bread. Sprinkle
cinnamon on after it is cooked and serve with butter and syrup.

Chile Relleno in a dish

4 oz. can Diced chilies
1 1/2 cups grated cheddar cheese
1 1/2 cups grated Monterey Jack cheese
7 or 8 eggs
13 oz. can evaporated milk

Mix all ingredients and pour into baking dish. Bake at 350 for 35 to 40 minutes.

A tall horse and low branches,
when combined, make loose teeth.

———◆◆◇◆◆———

A fool is someone who doesn't
know he doesn't know.

Anonymous

———◆◆◇◆◆———

The cowboy who can out work a cowgirl
can always choose his employer.

———◆◆◇◆◆———

13

Apple Oatmeal

2 tbsp butter
2 cups chopped apples
4 cups boiling water
2 cups raisins
2 cups nuts
4 cups old fashioned oats
2 2/3 cups non-fat dry milk
3/4 cup brown sugar
1 tbsp salt
2 tbsp cinnamon

Combine all ingredients and mix. Place in 9 by 13 casserole dish.
Bake uncovered at 350 for 30 to 35 minutes.

*Serve with half and half or buttermilk.

Shorty's Scramble

6 eggs
1/2 cup cooked sausage, ham or bacon pieces
1/2 bell pepper, chopped
1/2 onion, chopped
1 tomato, chopped
1/2 cup grated cheese
Salsa

Scramble eggs in mixing bowl and pour into greased frying pan. Cook over medium heat for 1 1/2 minutes, until eggs start to thicken. Add meat, pepper, onion, tomato and cheese. Mix and cook until eggs are cooked all the way. Top with salsa to taste.

Herman's German Pancakes

6 eggs
1 cup flour
1 cup milk
1/4 tbsp salt
5 tbsp butter

Blend in blender eggs, flour, milk and salt for about 2 minutes.
Melt butter in 9 by 13 pan and pour batter in. Bake at 450 for 15
to 20 minutes.

A bouquet of roses won't always get a cowboy out of deep trouble, but they will at least make the trouble shallower.

———◆►◄◆———

Chaps can't help you if you're riding backwards.

———◆►◄◆———

Although blood is thicker than water, sometimes even blood is thinner than money.

———◆►◄◆———

Lead Pancakes

One way or another, we'll fill your belly full of lead.

> 1 egg
> 1 cup whole milk*
> 2 tbsp melted shortening or vegetable oil
> 2/3 cup flour
> 2/3 cup rolled oats
> 2 tbsp brown sugar
> 1 tsp baking powder
> 1/2 tsp soda
> 1/2 tsp salt

Mix ingredients. Stir until smooth. Pour batter onto a hot, oiled griddle. Makes 4 6-inch pancakes.

*May substitute 1 1/4 cup buttermilk

You can always tell a cowboy, but you can't tell him much.

———◆▸◄◆◄◆———

The cowboy life is great for men and dogs, but hell on women and horses.

———◆▸◄◆◄◆———

If you plan to insult the chef, it's best to wait until you're finished eating.

———◆▸◄◆◄◆———

Rise 'n Shine Ham & Eggs

1 tbsp butter
2 slices of ham
2 eggs
1 tsp apple juice, cider or water

Melt the butter in a frying pan and lightly brown one side of the ham. Turn and break an egg on the other side. Sprinkle with pepper, no salt. Add apple juice or water and cover tightly. Cook until the egg whites are solid.

Potato Pancakes

4 medium potatoes, peeled and grated
1 onion, minced
2 tbsp flour
1/8 tsp nutmeg
1 egg, slightly beaten
1/2 tsp salt

Combine all ingredients, except potato, and mix. Add potato and fry in butter. Flatten mounds into 4 inch circles with pancake turner while cooking. Cooking time is approximately 5 minutes.

*For a yummy treat, top with apple sauce and sour cream.

Dripper Breakfast

3 cups cubed French bread
1 cup grated cheese
1/2 cup chopped onion
1/2 cup chopped green bell pepper
1 can mushrooms, drained
1/2 cup chopped tomatoes
10 eggs, beaten
4 cups milk
1 tsp prepared mustard
1 tsp salt
1/4 tsp onion powder
1/4 tsp pepper
10 slices crispy bacon, crumbled

Arrange bread in the bottom of a buttered 9 by 13 baking pan. Then layer with cheese, onion, bell pepper, mushrooms and tomato and set pan aside. In a large mixing bowl combine eggs, milk, mustard, salt, onion powder and pepper then pour over layers in the baking dish. Sprinkle bacon crumbles over top. Bake 1 hour and 15 minutes at 325.

*May be done ahead and stored in the fridge.

Stick to Yer Ribs Oatmeal

4 cups of your favorite cooked oatmeal
1 cup applesauce
1 tsp cinnamon

Stir applesauce and cinnamon into oatmeal and serve.

Or instead of applesauce and cinnamon, add 2/3 Cup raisins while the oatmeal is cooking.

A burr in your own saddle is a pain; a burr in someone else's saddle is entertainment.

———◆◆×◆◆———

No group of men ever had more time for thinking than cowboys.

———◆◆×◆◆———

If you don't want to smell like cedar smoke, don't hang around the campfire.

———◆◆×◆◆———

Whole Wheat Pancakes

For the hungry crowd who needs to work hard all day

   1 1/2 cup whole wheat
   2 cups sour milk or buttermilk
   1/2 cup butter
   2 tsp baking soda
   4 to 5 tbsp honey
   4 eggs
   4 tsp baking powder
   1/2 tsp salt

Blend all ingredients together in a blender and fry on a griddle.

Scones

2 cups milk
1/2 cup shortening
3 tbsp yeast
1/2 cup very warm water
1/2 cup sugar
3 eggs, beaten
1 tsp salt
6 to 7 cups flour

Add yeast to warm water and mix, then add sugar. Scald milk, then combine all ingredients together, including yeast mixture. Mix well. Roll out on floured surface and cut into squares. Fry in hot oil until browned on both sides.

Serve with jam or honey butter.

Honey Butter

1/2 cup butter, softened
1/2 cup honey
1/4 tsp vanilla

Whip butter and add vanilla. Gradually add honey while whipping mixture.

The Code of the West

After you pass some one on the trail, don't look
back at him. It implies you don't trust him.

Don't complain. Complaining is what quitters do,
and cowboys hate quitters.

Never even bother another man's horse.

Cuss all you want…but only around men,
horses and cows.

Never wake another man by shaking or touching him;
He might wake up suddenly and shoot you.

A cowboy doesn't talk much;
he saves his breath for breathing.

Never pass anyone on the trail
without saying "Howdy."

29

Dinners & Main Dishes

If it doesn't taste like pork, beef, or chicken, you probably don't want to know what it is, so don't ask or you just might find out.

When cowboys were out herding cattle on the range or on a cattle drive, beef cows were everywhere; however, the beef was rarely for them. Cowboys were usually taking the cattle to be sold. Cattle would bring a fair price at market, so they were too valuable to eat along the way. The only time the cowboys ate beef was when a cow died or became lame or something else happened that would make it worthless at market. As a result, cowboys often used other kinds of meat instead to make their tasty meals.

I have included some beef recipes for the benefit of the cowboys of today who love a good meal with beef as a main dish.

Tiny's Venison Stew

1/4 lb salt pork, trimmed
2 lbs. boneless venison, trimmed
1/2 cup flour
1 cup onions
1/2 tsp garlic
2 cups chicken stock
1 bay leaf, crumbled
1/2 tsp thyme, crumbled
1 tsp salt
1/4 tsp black pepper
4 medium potatoes, peeled and quartered
2 medium carrots
2 tbsp distilled white vinegar

Before you start cooking anything, cut pork into 1/4 inch cubes and venison into 2 inch cubes. Finely chop onions and garlic. Peel and quarter potatoes and scrape carrots and cut into 2 inch lengths.

Fry pork over medium heat in a heavy 4 to 5 qt casserole. Stir pieces until they are crisp and brown. Transfer to separate dish to drain. Save 4 Tbsp of fat from pan and drain the rest. Evenly coat the venison in flour. Brown over high heat in pork fat, 4 or 5 pieces at a time. Turn cubes occasionally so they brown evenly. Set aside cooked venison cubes on separate plate. Add onions and garlic to casserole and cook and stir for 5 minutes or until they're soft and translucent, do not brown. Pour in stock and bring to a boil. Add bay leaf, thyme, salt and pepper and cooked venison. Reduce to low heat and cover tightly. Simmer for 1 hour. Add potatoes and carrots to casserole and moisten evenly. Continue to simmer covered for 20 to 30 minutes or until vegetables are tender. Stir in vinegar. Sprinkle pork bits on top and serve at once.

Aunt Phoebe's Goulash

This is one of my dad's favorite meals. "There's nothing better than a bowl of hot goulash on a cold day."

1 lb. ground beef
1 onion-diced
1 cup cooked elbow noodles
1 qt. stewed tomatoes
1 qt. tomato juice
1 tbsp Worcestershire sauce
1 tbsp mustard
salt and pepper to taste
1 cup grated cheese

Boil noodles in 3 Cups water until tender, do not drain. In separate pan, brown ground beef and onion. Stir together tomatoes and juice, Worcestershire sauce, mustard, salt and pepper and bring to a low boil. Add meat and noodles and simmer for five minutes. Stir in cheese.

Serves 6.

Soreness in ribs miraculously cured by the dance floor will return promptly when chores begin.

———◆◆)◆(◆◆———

It does no good to nail shoes onto hooves that are already sore.

———◆◆)◆(◆◆———

Never leave your favorite magazine in the outhouse.

———◆◆)◆(◆◆———

Rabbit Stew

meat of a rabbit
1 large onion
1 celery stalk
salt and pepper
carrots
potatoes
flour
cold water

Cut meat into chunks, dice onion, and chop celery and put into a heavy kettle. Bring water to a boil then pour in over rabbit and veggies. Simmer for about 2 hours. While it is simmering, slice up carrots and cube potatoes. If you want a lot of stew, use a lot of carrots and potatoes (if you want not so much stew, only use a few carrots and potatoes). Add carrots and potatoes to stew and simmer until vegetables are tender. Mix flour and water to form a paste and add to stew to thicken if desired.

Poor Man's Sausage Soup

4 slices bacon, cut up
1 cup chopped onions
1 cup sliced carrots
1 cup chopped celery
16 oz lentils
3 quarts water
2 tbsp vinegar
1 tbsp beef stock or 2 beef bullion cubes
2 tsp dry mustard
2 cups frankfurters or vienna sausage
1/4 cup catsup
1 tsp salt
1/4 tsp pepper
1/4 cup red wine (optional)

Fry bacon until partially done. Add vegetables and sauté for 5 minutes. Add lentils, water, vinegar, beef stock and mustard. Bring to a boil and cover. Reduce heat and simmer for 1 hour. Add frankfurters, catsup, salt and pepper. Simmer for 15 to 20 minutes. Add wine just before serving.

Texas Beans

6 slices bacon
1/2 cup finely chopped onion
1/2 cup chopped celery
3 cups cooked green beans
8 ounces tomato sauce
1 tsp Worcestershire sauce
salt and pepper
1/2 cup buttered bread crumbs

Sauté bacon, onion and celery. Combine with beans, tomato
sauce, Worcestershire sauce, salt and pepper. Put into greased 1
1/2 qt casserole dish. Sprinkle buttered crumbs over the top and
bake uncovered at 375 for 20 minutes.

Traditional Chicken Fried Steak

1 1/2 lbs beef round steak, 1/2 inch thick
1 egg, beaten
1 tbsp milk
1 cup fine cracker crumbs
1/4 cup salad oil

Pound steak to 1/4 inch thick and cut into pieces. Blend egg and milk together. Dip meat pieces in mixture, then into bread crumbs. Slowly brown meat in hot oil, turning once. Cover and cook over low heat 45 to 60 minutes or until tender. Season to taste.

Your horse will always walk the fastest when she's headed home.

———◆◆×◆◆———

The older the horse, the more enthusiastic the seller.

———◆◆×◆◆———

A man's best hairpiece is a ten-gallon hat.

———◆◆×◆◆———

Fernando's Hot Caldo Con Queso

Intended to feed a group of 8 hungry cowboys and their ladies.

2 1/2 cups water
4 oz diced green chilies
1 large tomato-peeled and diced
1 tsp garlic salt
1/4 tsp pepper
13 oz evaporated milk*
10 3/4 oz can of cream of potato soup*
10 3/4 oz can of cream of onion soup*
Monterey Jack cheese-cubed

Combine water, chilies, tomatoes, garlic salt, and pepper. Bring to a boil, cover and simmer for 5 minutes. Blend in evaporated milk, soups and heat thoroughly. Pour over cubes of cheese.

*Aren't you glad that we have prepared foods now so that the more modern cowboys can eat good food, and it's a bit easier to prepare than it was for our predecessors.

Jim-Bob's Noodle Mixins

2 lbs. ground beef
2 medium onions-chopped
1 garlic clove-crushed
14 oz spaghetti sauce
1 lb stewed tomatoes
1 can mushrooms
8 oz shell or elbow noodles
1 1/2 pints sour cream
16 oz mozzarella cheese

Brown ground beef and onions in skillet. Drain and add garlic, spaghetti sauce, tomatoes and un-drained mushrooms. Mix well and simmer for 20 minutes. Cook noodles according to directions on package and drain well. Layer noodles, meat sauce, sour cream and cheese. Cover and bake at 350 for 35 to 40 minutes. Then bake uncovered until cheese is slightly browned.

God must have loved calories;
he made so many of them.

Anonymous

———◆━━◆◆━◆———

A tumbleweed has no social life.

———◆━━◆◆━◆———

If you find that the coyotes join in whenever
you sing, try the harmonica.

———◆━━◆◆━◆———

Brian's Dutch Oven Beans

1 lb bacon
1 onion, chopped
5 cans pork and beans
2 to 2 1/2 Cups brown sugar

Slice bacon into squares, fry with chopped onion. Add pork and beans and brown sugar. Pour into Dutch Oven and cook until heated through.

Trail Beans

2 cups pinto beans
pinch of baking soda
salt pork

Place beans in large cooking pot and cover with water. Let stand over night. Drain beans, then cover beans again with water. Add baking soda and bring to a boil. Reduce heat and simmer for one to two hours, until skin of bean splits when you blow on it. Add pork and season to taste.

*Season with paprika for a kick.

Pear Pork Chops

4 pork chops
vegetable oil
1/4 tsp salt
1/4 tsp black pepper
2 medium pears
2 tbsp butter
1 tbsp green peppercorns, crushed
1/4 cup crumbled blue cheese

Brush pork chops lightly with vegetable oil and season with salt
and pepper. Cook chops in a large skillet for 4 to 5 minutes on
each side. Remove chops from skillet and keep warm. Cut pears
in half, core and cut into thin slices. Cook pears in the skillet for 1
minute with butter. Stir in peppercorns and cook while stirring for
2 minutes. Spoon pears over chips and sprinkle with blue cheese.

God does not hold men accountable for the cussing done at cows.

The warmer the bedroll, the friendlier the snakes.

A whistlin' cowboy can't stay mad.

Never give an angry woman bad news.

———◆◆✕◆●———

The best way to make a small fortune gambling
is to start out with a big fortune.
Anonymous

———◆◆✕◆●———

A true cowboy is half stubbornness, half grit, half
gentleman, and all courage.

———◆◆✕◆●———

Long-Riders' Stuffed Zucchini

2 large zucchinis
1 lb ground beef
1/2 onion
cooked rice
1 egg
1 can Cream of Mushroom soup
1 tsp cloves
salt and pepper

Brown hamburger and onions. Add rice, egg, soup, cloves, salt and pepper. Hollow out center of zucchinis and stuff with mixture. Put water in the bottom of a dripper pan and place zucchinis in water. Bake at 350 for 1 hour.

Old Time Trail Mincemeat

Especially popular around the holidays.

2 lbs cooked venison*, cooled and chopped in food grinder
4 1/2 lbs apples
4 cups brown sugar
2 lbs raisins
1 lb currants
3/4 lbs butter
1/2 tsp nutmeg
1/2 tsp cloves
1 tsp mace
2 tsp salt
1 tsp cinnamon
apple cider

Combine all ingredients. Put in large skillet and cover with cider. Cook over low heat until tender.

*Beef can also be used.

No matter how much you water it, a cactus will never grow into a cottonwood tree.

———◆▸✕◂◆———

Oversee your workmen. If they be boys, separate them; for it is true: one boy is a boy, two boys are a half a boy; but three boys are no boy at all.

The Old Farmer's Almanac

———◆▸✕◂◆———

If you did it, try really hard not to draw attention to yourself and try not to look guilty while leaving quickly.

———◆▸✕◂◆———

Gus' Baked Beans

Especially for those evenings you're planning to have music after dinner.

1 qt beans
3 slices bacon
1/3 cup molasses
1 onion
1 bell pepper
1 tsp mustard
1 small can chunked pineapple
1 to 1 1/2 cups brown sugar

Mix all ingredients in a saucepan and cook on medium heat until just before it boils.

Hank's Pheasant & Mushrooms

1 whole pheasant or chicken, cut into pieces
1 tsp. fresh thyme, chopped
salt and pepper
olive oil as needed
3 tbsp. Brandy
2 large garlic cloves, minced
2 bay leaves
1/2 cup white wine
1 cup good stock
   (chicken broth can be used in a pinch)
1 cup whipping cream
1 lb. wild mushrooms
   (Shitake, Oyster or Chanterelles work well)
butter as needed
1 tbsp. chopped parsley

Sprinkle bird with thyme, salt and pepper. Saute in hot oil until golden brown. Remove from pan and pour off oil. Return bird to pan. Turn on to medium heat. Add brandy, Stand back and ignite. (If using gas cook top, quickly move pan back and forth and Brandy will ignite. If using other cook top, stand a safe distance away and toss a match into pan and don't forget to remove the matchstick). After flames die down, add garlic, bay leaves, wine, stock and cream. Simmer covered for 1 hour. While pheasant is simmering, sauté mushrooms in butter and add to bird for the last 10 minutes. Serve over rice or noodles.

The dustier the trail, the thicker the soup.

A fool and his money are some party.
Wyoming Bumper Sticker

A persnickety horse makes for a long ride.

Will's Scalloped Mushrooms

1 lb fresh mushrooms- sliced
2 cups soft bread crumbs
1/2 cup melted butter
1/3 cup dry white wine
salt and pepper

Butter 1 1/2 quart casserole dish. Layer twice starting with mushrooms, bread crumbs, butter and sprinkle with salt and pepper. Pour wine over top and cover. Bake at 325 for 25 minutes. Combine remaining butter and bread crumbs and sprinkle over top. Bake uncovered for 10 more minutes, or until crumbs are lightly toasted.

Ellis' Lake Trout

This is my grandpa's recipe for trout. He grew up on a farm in Central Utah doing what cowboys do; riding horses, mending fences, herding cattle and digging ditches (he also did a little farming on the side).

1 cup flour
salt and pepper
freshly caught trout
bacon grease

Clean the trout, remove heads and tails and rinse well. Put flour and salt and pepper in a plastic bag. Drop trout into bag and shake well until fish is completely coated. Heat cast iron grill over an open fire. Melt ample bacon drippings; when grease is hot, spread fish open and place belly down on grill. Over an open fire, fry each side until browned. A 12 inch trout usually takes about 10 minutes to cook fully.

It is very important to control the heat on the grill. If grill gets too hot, move or raise it to change temperature.
*Serve with a lemon wedge or tartar sauce.

A cowboy is bound to respect virtuous
womanhood, trustworthy manhood, the
democratic process, and anyone
with a loaded gun.

———◆◆✕◆———

A rancher doesn't worry too much about his
"cash flow" because he knows that one direction
or another, somehow it always will.

———◆◆✕◆———

The hungrier the cowboy, the tastier the food.

———◆◆✕◆———

Grampa's Deep Fried Fish Fillet

This is the in-the-kitchen version of the Lake trout.

1 cup flour
salt and pepper
whole trout or bass
cooking oil

Clean fish, remove heads and tails and rinse well. Run sharp fillet knife just under skin and peel skin off. Split fish into two fillets by cutting alongside the back bone (it isn't necessary to remove bones, as they become brittle during cooking). Cut large fish into smaller pieces. Mix flour, salt and pepper in a bowl and dip fish fillets in mix. Heat large, deep frying pan and add enough cooking oil to cover fish. When oil is hot, carefully place fish into hot oil. Fry 2 to 3 Minutes or until cooked through.

Range-Rider Cowboy Pie

Also known as Shepherd's Pie, but if you call it that, you won't be able to get any self-respecting cowboy to eat it.

10 ounces gravy
1 cup roast lamb or beef
3/4 cup sliced carrots
1/2 cup chopped onions
1/2 cup chopped celery
1/2 cup frozen peas
salt and pepper
3 cups mashed potatoes
1/2 cup grated cheese

Parboil carrots, onions and celery. Drain and add gravy, meat and peas. Salt and pepper to taste. Put mixture in 8 by 8 inch baking dish. Spread mashed potatoes over top and sprinkle cheese over it. Bake at 350 until cheese is melted and mixture is bubbling.

When in doubt, let your horse do the thinking.
Old cowboy saying

————◆►✖◄◆————

The only man a cowboy fears is a wo-man.

————◆►✖◄◆————

It's always easiest to pound a nail that's never
been bent.

————◆►✖◄◆————

Dwayne's Famous Meat Loaf

2 lbs ground beef
1 onion-chopped
1 bell pepper-chopped
2 to 3 packages saltine crackers
milk

Brown ground beef and add onions, peppers, crackers and enough milk to moisten it. Bake in a casserole dish at 325-350 for 1 1/2 to 2 hours.

Lyin' Around Soup

4 small carrots- sliced crosswise
2 new potatoes- diced
1 small cauliflower
3/4 cup fresh green peas
1/2 cup fresh string beans- cut into strips
4 small radishes- halved
2 tsp salt
1/4 lb fresh spinach- finely chopped
2 tbsp butter
1 egg yolk
2 tbsp flour
1 cup milk
1/4 tsp white pepper
1/4 cup heavy cream

Put carrots, potatoes, cauliflower, peas, beans and radishes in a pot and cover with water. Add salt and boil for 5 minutes or until vegetables are tender. Add spinach and boil 5 more minutes. Strain liquid into a bowl and set aside. Melt butter in separate pan. Remove from heat and add flour. Beating constantly, pour in stock and milk. Combine cream and egg yolk. Stirring constantly, gradually add 1 cup of hot liquid to egg mixture. Beat into soupy mixture. Add vegetables and simmer. Season with white pepper and serve immediately.

Whenever you give someone a piece of your mind, be sure you can get along on what's left.

Anonymous

———◆◆◆◆———

If you want good hard calluses, you must first endure a few blisters.

———◆◆◆◆———

When the chips are down, the bull is empty

Montana Bumper Sticker

———◆◆◆◆———

Doc's Dutch-Oven Corned Beef

3 to 4 lb corned beef brisket
1/2 cup chopped onion
2 garlic cloves, minced
2 bay leaves
6 medium potatoes, pared
6 small carrots, pared
6 cabbage wedges
prepared mustard (optional)
1/4 cup brown sugar (optional)
dash ground cloves (optional)

Place corned beef in Dutch oven and barely cover with hot water. Add onion, garlic and bay leaves. Cover and simmer 3 to 4 hours, until tender. Remove meat from liquid and keep warm. Add potatoes and carrots; cover and bring to a boil. Cook 10 minutes. Add cabbage and cook 20 minutes longer.

Optional glaze: glaze meat while vegetables cook. Spread fat side of meat lightly with prepared mustard. Sprinkle with mixture of brown sugar and cloves. Bake at 350 in shallow pan for 15 to 20 minutes.

Campfire Trout

trout or salmon
Miracle Whip
salt and pepper
lemon juice

Clean fish thoroughly. Smear entire fish with miracle whip and season with salt, pepper and lemon juice. Wrap in aluminum foil and seal all edges to keep juices inside. Place on hot coals or bar-beque. Cover fish package with lid on barbeque. Cook unattended until done. Trout usually takes 6 to 8 minutes, Salmon takes 12 to 15 minutes.

If you watch the rider behind you, he will catch you; if you watch the rider ahead, you may discover why he's ahead.

———◆◆×◆◆———

The bravery of a cowboy has a lot to do with the speed of his horse.

———◆◆×◆◆———

There is no nose so pretty it looks good in someone else's business.

Old Country Saying

———◆◆×◆◆———

Oatmeal Venison Patties

6 slices bacon, cut in squares
1 lb ground venison
1 lb ground pork
1 cup canned tomatoes
1 egg
1 tbsp onions, chopped
1/4 cup oatmeal
salt and pepper

Line muffin tins with bacon pieces. Combine remaining ingredients and mix well. Spoon mixture into tins and bake at 350 for 50 minutes.

Why do Cowboys wear what they do?

The reasons why cowboys dress the way they do quickly become obvious to anyone as soon as he saddles up. Philip Ashton Rollins said about cowboy's clothing, "A cowboy's clothing, though picturesque, was not worn for effect. It was simply best suited for the work at hand."

Most cowboys won't last long under the baking sun without a good hat; a nice tall ten gallon with the widest rim he can find usually works best to keep out sun, rain, snow and whatever else mother nature decides to hurl at him. A cowboy's hat was so important to him, that in the Old West, there was Cowboy Hat Etiquette, stating things like, "Don't try on another man's hat. It's almost as bad as getting on his horse," and, "Never put your hat on a bed or bunk; that's bad luck".

A handkerchief is the only thing that can keep the dust out of your mouth and nose on a windy day. In fact, windy days aren't the only days there's dust in the air. It's everywhere, all the time. Dust gets in your mouth, in your nose, ears, eyes, hair, clothes, in between your fingers and toes, I'm telling you, it gets EVERYWHERE. A belt buckle is a must to be an authentic cowboy; no one will believe he's a real cowboy if he's not sporting a gold belt buckle at least the size of his head.

Next in the cowboy wardrobe are chaps. A man not wearing chaps, after riding for a few feet through the brush, finds trickles of blood running down his legs from thorns and stickers, not to mention ripped, filthy blue jeans. The chaps then get tucked into boots that fit snugly into the stirrups and help keep him from falling off when the pony he's riding decides to throw him.

A saddle wasn't part of a cowboy's clothes, but it was absolutely essential to the cowboy. Next to a cowboy's horse, his saddle was probably the most important thing he owned. His rear end spent many long hours in that seat; if the saddle wasn't just right, then the next day, the cowboy would be walking even funnier than usual.

Along with their garb and gear, cowboys lived by the Code of the West. If a cowboy was to survive the life of the West, he had to have at least some knowledge of the rules of the Code.

Breads

Real cowboys and their way of life are vanishing from the West. There are not nearly as many as there used to be; however, you can still find 'em scattered throughout the West and Southwest. If you're looking, they are still rounding up and herding the cows, keeping up the ranches and doing whatever else the cowboy decides to do.

Cowboy Coffee Can Cake

1 cup sifted flour
1 tsp. baking powder
1 tsp. soda
1 tsp. salt
1 cup corn meal
1 cup stirred whole wheat flour
3/4 cup dark molasses
1 cup nuts (optional)
2 cups buttermilk or sour milk
1 cup raisins

Sift together: flour, baking powder, soda and salt. Stir in cornmeal and whole wheat flour. Add remaining ingredients and beat well. Pout batter into a greased 3 lb. coffee can. Pour 2 cups of water into a crock pot and set coffee can inside. Lay aluminum foil over the top of can and cooker and fold down around edges of crock pot. Bake covered on high for 4 to 5 hours. Remove and let cool for 1 hour before unmolding. Slice and serve.

This bread is real yummy served with cream cheese.

Raid the Hive Honey Bread

1 1/2 cups honey
3/4 cups sugar
1 1/2 cups milk
1 1/2 tsp baking soda
3 3/4 cups flour
1/3 cup cooking oil
1 1/2 tsp salt
1 tsp vanilla
2 eggs
1 1/2 cups chopped nuts

Bring honey, milk and sugar to a boil. Cool. Sift dry ingredients together, add nuts shortening, eggs and vanilla. Add the cooled honey mixture and beat for 2 minutes. Turn into well greased pans. Bake at 355 for 1 hour.

Cowboy's Cake

2 1/2 cups flour
2 cups brown sugar
1/2 tsp. salt
2/3 cups shortening
2 tsp. baking powder
1/2 tsp. soda
1/2 tsp. cinnamon
1/2 tsp. nutmeg
1 cup sour milk
1 beaten egg

Mix flour, sugar, salt and shortening until crumbly. Save 1/2 cup of the crumbs to sprinkle on top. To remaining crumbs, add baking powder, baking soda and other spices and mix well. Add milk and eggs, and mix well. Pour into greased and floured 9x13" pan. Sprinkle remaining crumbs on top. Bake at 350 for 25 to 30 minutes. Serve warm and buttered.

Annie's Whole Wheat Muffins

1/2 cup margarine
1 cup brown sugar
1 egg
1 cup milk
1 tsp vanilla
2 cups wheat flour
4 tsp baking powder
1/2 cups nuts

Cream butter and sugar. Add egg, milk and flour alternately. Bake in muffin tin at 425 for 12-15 minutes.

Six Weeks on the Trail Muffins

2 cups boiling water
5 cups whole wheat flour
1 1/2 tsp salt
1 cup wheat germ
1 cup honey or molasses
4 cups buttermilk or yogurt
5 cups bran
5 tsp baking soda
2 tsp cinnamon
1 cup oil
4 eggs, beaten
1 cup dates, raisins or chopped apple

Pour boiling water over 2 cups bran. In another bowl, sift flour, soda, salt, and spice. Add wheat germ and remaining bran. Combine with wet bran. Stir until moist. Add oil, honey, eggs, buttermilk and fruit or nuts. Pour into well greased muffin tins. Bake at 400 for 15-20 minutes. Keep in refrigerator to use as needed.

Frenchy's Zucchini Bread

3 eggs, well beaten
1 cup oil
2 cups sugar
2 cups raw grated zucchini
3 tsp vanilla
3 cups flour
1 tsp baking soda
1 tsp salt
3 tsp cinnamon
1/4 tsp baking powder

Combine eggs, oil, sugar, zucchini and vanilla. Mix well. Sift flour, soda and salt and mix. Combine wet and dry ingredients and mix well. Bake at 350 for 60 minutes.

The only time a woman can change a man is when he's a baby.

Anonymous

—◆◆✕◆●—

If it's free, don't complain.

—◆◆✕◆●—

You never have to wonder if people just like you for your money when you drive an old pickup.

—◆◆✕◆●—

John's Baking Powder Biscuits

2 cups flour
2 1/2 tsp baking powder
1/2 tsp salt
1/3 cup shortening
2/3 to 1 cup milk

Combine flour, baking powder and salt. Add shortening and cut into flour with fork. Make mixture into a bowl shape with middle hollowed out in bowl. add milk by pouring into middle of bowl then tossing mixture on top of milk. Mix as little as possible, only until it makes a soft ball. It should not be smooth. Knead, no more than 8 times. Pat or roll out. Cut circles with cookie cutter. Dip in butter. Cook at 425 for 12-15 minutes.

Chuck Wagon Noodles

1 egg
1/2 tsp salt (optional)
2 tbsp water or milk
1 to 1 1/4 cups whole wheat flour
   (white flour may be substituted for wheat, or
   use half wheat and half white)

Generously flour your working surface. Combine all ingredients and add enough flour to make dough stiff. Place dough on floured surface and roll out until very thin. Cut into strips about 1/4" wide and let dry for about 2 hours. Drop into boiling soup or boiling, salted water and cook uncovered about 10 minutes. Makes 3 cups cooked noodles.

Aunt Polly's Dumplings

pinch of salt
1 cup flour
1 tsp baking powder
1 tbsp butter
1/2 cup milk
1 egg (optional)

Mix top ingredients together like a pie crust. Then mix all ingredients together. Drop spoonfuls into your favorite soup. Cover. Cook until centers are not doughy.

Slim's Corn Bread

1 cup yellow cornmeal
1 cup flour
2 tbsp sugar
4 tsp baking powder
1/2 tsp salt
1 cup milk
1/4 cup shortening
1 egg

Preheat oven to 425. Grease square 8x8 or 9x9 pan. Blend all ingredients for 20 seconds. Then beat vigorously for 1 min. Pour into prepared pan. Bake at 425 for 20 to 25 minutes or until golden brown.

Desserts

Life is short. Eat dessert first.

- From a billboard in Wyoming

Best Durn Yellow Cake Ever

    2 1/2 cups flour
    2 1/4 tsp baking powder
    1/4 tsp salt
    1 1/4 cups sugar
    1 1/2 cups shortening
    1 1/2 tsp vanilla
    2 eggs
    1 cup milk

Cream sugar and shortening on low speed. Add vanilla. Add eggs
1 at a time. Combine flour, baking powder and salt in separate
bowl. Alternately add milk and dry ingredients to sugar mixture,
begin and end with dry. Beat for 1 minute. Divide into 2 pans.
Bake on 375 for 20 minutes.

Sugar Cookies For Your Sweetie

3 cups sugar
1 pint sour cream
1 tsp soda
6 tsp baking powder
1/2 cup butter
pinch of salt
4 eggs
2 tsp vanilla
8 cups flour

Combine all ingredients in large bowl. Mix until well blended.
Roll into ball and wrap with plastic wrap. Refrigerate for 2 hours.
Roll out until it is a cylinder about 2 to 3 inches thick. Cut slices
and put on greased cookie sheet. Bake at 375 for 7 minutes.

Ponies with broken spirits don't win races.

———◆▸✖◂◆———

Shoveling dirt out back is work; somehow, doing
the same thing at the beach is play.
What's the difference?

———◆▸✖◂◆———

It's easy for the watchdog to get distracted when
he's having his belly scratched.

———◆▸✖◂◆———

Betsy's Buttermilk Cookies

A favorite of cowboys after a long ride.

    1/2 cup shortening
    1/2 cup butter
    1 1/2 cups sugar
    2 eggs
    1 cup buttermilk
    1 tsp vanilla
    3 cups + 3 tsp flour
    1 tsp baking soda
    1/2 tsp baking powder
    1/2 tsp salt

Mix shortening, butter, sugar and eggs. Stir in buttermilk and vanilla. Then add flour, soda, baking powder and salt. Bake at 375 for 10 minutes.

Bucked Off Banana Cookies

3/4 cup shortening
1 1/4 cups rolled oats
1 cup sugar
3/4 tsp cinnamon
3 mashed bananas
1 1/2 cup flour
1 egg
1/2 tsp baking soda
1 tsp salt
1 cup chocolate chips

Combine all ingredients and mix until well blended. Bake at 350 for 12-15 minutes.

When a man gets too big for his britches usually his backside will be all that's showing.

————◆◆►◄◆————

No matter how innocent she may look, a cow is always up to no good.

————◆◆►◄◆————

Having only one suit of clothes makes the choice of what to wear simple.

————◆◆►◄◆————

Maria's Flan de Carmelo

A south of the border sweet treat.

- **1 1/2 cups sugar**
- **6 eggs**
- **2 cans evaporated milk**
- **1 tsp vanilla**
- **pinch of salt**

Melt 1/2 cup sugar in a frying pan and pour into bottom of a
9 x 13 pan. Blend all remaining ingredients and pour into pan.
Bake in another pan of water at 350 for one hour.

Arroz Con Leche

Traditional Rice Pudding with a zing.

1 cup cooked rice
3 eggs- beaten
1/4 cup sugar
1/2 tsp vanilla
2 1/2 cups milk
1/4 cup raisins
sprinkle of cinnamon

Mix all ingredients together and pour into a 9x13 pan. Sprinkle with nutmeg. Put pan in another dish of water. Bake at 350 for 60 to 90 minutes, or until set.

There's no accountin' for taste.

Old-Time Saying

———◆◆◆◆◆———

The best place to work has always been the one with spectacular vistas, no walls, no time clocks, and no traffic jams.

———◆◆◆◆◆———

Worry is like a rocking chair; it gives you something to do but doesn't get you anywhere.

Anonymous

———◆◆◆◆◆———

Mom's Raisin Spice Cake

2 cups raisins
2 cups water
1 cup cold water
1/2 cup lard
2 cups sugar
1 tsp salt
1 tsp cinnamon
1 tsp cloves
1 tsp nutmeg
1 tbsp soda dissolved in a little hot water
4 cups flour

Simmer raisins and water for 15 minutes. Add rest of water, lard, sugar, salt, cinnamon, cloves, nutmeg, soda and flour and mix. Pour into a greased 9x13 pan. Bake at 350 for 60 minutes.

Optional: Frost with white frosting or sprinkle with powdered sugar.

Redheaded Cowgirl Carrot Cake

1 cup sugar
2 cups flour
1 tsp baking powder
2 tsp cinnamon
1 cup brown sugar
1 1/4 tsp baking soda
1 tsp salt
1 cup vegetable oil
3 cups grated carrots
1 cup raisins
4 eggs
1 cup chopped nuts
1/2 cup chocolate chips

Thoroughly mix sugars, flour, baking powder, cinnamon, soda and salt. Then add vegetable oil, carrots, raisins, eggs, nuts and chocolate chips. Pour into 2 greased loaf pans. Bake at 300 for 65 minutes.

Odds & Ends

When a man's head gets too big for his hat,
it usually takes a woman
to know the best ways to shrink it.

Cowboy Cider

1 cup sugar
3 cups water
12 whole cloves
4 all spice berries
2 or 3 sticks of cinnamon
1/2 tsp ginger
3 cups orange juice
8 cups apple cider
2 cups lemon juice

Boil sugar and water for 10 minutes. Add cloves, berries, cinnamon and ginger. Cover and let stand for 1 hour. Strain and then add orange juice, apple cider and lemon juice. Bring to a light boil and serve.

The dinner bell is always in tune.
Old-Time Saying

———◆◆►◄◆◆———

If you want fresh, clean oats, you have to pay a fair price; if getting a low price is all that matters, you must be content with oats that have already passed through the horse.
Sign on a feed store wall

———◆◆►◄◆◆———

The only sure thing about a man's fortune is that it is always about to change.

———◆◆►◄◆◆———

7 Day Sweet Pickles

14 medium size cucumbers
2/3 quart vinegar
1/2 quart water
8 cups sugar
2 tbsp salt
25 whole cloves
3 cinnamon sticks
green coloring

Slice cucumbers and, in glass container, cover with boiling water each day for four days. Each day, pour water off and rinse cukes with cool water and rinse out container. On the 5th day, combine vinegar, water, sugar, salt, cloves, cinnamon and coloring. Pour over cukes. For the next 2 days, reheat to boiling and pour over cukes. On the 7th day, pour into sterilized jars and seal tightly.

Big Bull BBQ Sauce

1 cup catsup
2 tsp mustard
1/2 cup brown sugar
1 tsp diced onions
1/4 tsp salt
1/2 tsp minced garlic
2 capfuls lemon juice
1 capful Worcestershire sauce
1/2 cup chili sauce
1 tbsp butter

Cook in saucepan on medium heat until slightly thickened.

It's better to keep your mouth shut and have people wonder if you're a fool than to open your mouth and remove all doubt.

Old Time Saying

The reason why worry kills more people than work is because more people worry than work.

Sign on feed store wall

A frost-covered outhouse yields few splinters.

99

Recipe Notes:

Recipe Notes:

Order these additional Cookbooks from The American Pantry Collection

All cookbooks are $9.95 US.

Order Online! www.apricotpress.com

Apricot Press Order Form

Book Title	Quantity	x	Cost / Book	=	Total
_____	_____		_____		_____
_____	_____		_____		_____
_____	_____		_____		_____
_____	_____		_____		_____
_____	_____		_____		_____
_____	_____		_____		_____
_____	_____		_____		_____
_____	_____		_____		_____
_____	_____		_____		_____

Do not send Cash. Mail check or money order to:
Apricot Press   P.O. Box 1611
American Fork, Utah   84003
Telephone 801-756-0456
Allow 3 weeks for delivery.

Quantity discounts available.
Call us for more information.
9 a.m. - 5 p.m. MST

Sub Total =

Shipping = $2.00

Tax 8.5% =

Total Amount
Enclosed =

Shipping Address

Name:

Street:

City: State:

Zip Code:

Telephone:

Email: